Anglo
Saxon
Riddles

ANGLO-SAXON
RIDDLES

with
an introduction
and translations
from the
EXETER BOOK
by

Louis J Rodrigues

Copyright © Louis J Rodrigues, 1990.
Published by
LLANERCH ENTERPRISES.

ISBN 0947992464

PREFACE

The selection for treatment in this non-academic edition of only sixty riddles from the Exeter Book out of a possible ninety-five must seem somewhat arbitrary - and so it is. The thirty-five riddles omitted from this selection are either too short (some barely a line long), or too diffuse, fragmentary, or mutilated beyond recognition, in Latin, or else the subject of separate treatment in my projected series of **Anglo-Saxon verse Specimens rendered into Modern English.**

My preference for the terms "Anglo-Saxon" instead of "Old English" and "render" instead of "translate," represents the compromise I feel must be effected betwen historical fact and simple reality. Whether we call the original form of the language we speak today "Anglo-Saxon" or "Old English," it is sufficiently remote from modern usage in its orthography, syntax, and even vocabulary, to be considered necessary to "translate." And yet, for the very reason that it is the historical predecessor of Modern English, one would expect, instead, to have it "rendered" out of its antique state into its present-day equivalent.

In my rendering into Modern English of the following sixty riddles, I have endeavoured to retain those Anglo-Saxon lexical items that have survived into the modern period, albeit now regarded as obsolescent, or strictly poetical, in an effort to maintain the atmosphere of the original as also to emphasise the historical continuity of the language.

To enable the reader to perceive and appreciate this relationship with little difficulty, the Anglo-Saxon texts are printed alongside their Modern English renderings, and solutions to each of the riddles are offered in the design of the initial letters of the latter. A list of these solutions is appended for the convenience of the reader.

Since its conception, nine years ago, the project has suffered various vicissitudes. To begin with, Dave Thompson, the first illustrator, was able to produce only about twenty-six definitive designs before he ran out of ideas for the rest - although he left me with about eight further rough sketches for my consideration. Then, after a delay of approximately three years in obtaining the originals of the twenty-six illustrations, to replace the photostats I had been sent, a well-meaning collaborator disappeared with them to Mexico and repeated attempts to recover them, since, have failed. It was left to my elder son, Gavin, to reproduce Dave Thompson's work from these photostats and to complete the remaining thirty-four, using his imagination and relying, to a great extent, on my description of what was needed for each riddle. The difference in their styles is immediately noticeable but can hardly be helped. One could not have expected better from a then sixteen-year old.

I owe my abiding interest in Anglo-Saxon (whether it be prose or verse) to those under whom I was fortunate to study it - Professors Gavin Cochrane Martin at Madras, G N Garmonsway at London, and Peter Clemoes at Cambridge. The first two have been dead for some years now; but, both of them read with interest and criticized constructively my earliest "renderings" of **The Wanderer** and **The Dream of the Rood.**

In having the patience to endure my tantrums over the years since the manuscript was first produced, my thanks are due of course to my wife, Josefina, and to my second son, Marc.

LJR, Barcelona/Cambridge, 1990.

CONTENTS

Introduction   9

The Riddles:

    Natural Phenomena, 1, 2, 29, 33, 39, 50   19

    Chiefly Christian 6, 11, 43, 48, 55, 66   29

    Birds 7, 8, 9, 13, 57   39

    Animals 12, 15, 38   49

    Domestic Subjects 4,21,34,49,56,58,65,91 53

    Writing 26, 47, 51   67

    Music 31, 70   71

    Weapons & Fighting 5, 17, 23, 35   75

    Horn 14, 80   83

    Miscellaneous 10, 16, 22, 27, 28,
              32, 46, 52, 74, 85, 86   87

    Runes 24, 42, 64   105

    Obscene 25, 37, 44, 45, 54, 61, 62   109

Suggested Solutions   117

INTRODUCTION

Riddling is a universal phenomenon with a noble and ancient lineage. The Vedas, the Koran, the Old Testament, classical Greek literature, all abound in examples of riddles; and, there is none better known than that of the Sphinx, concerning the three ages of man. What is striking about some of these riddles is their similarity of theme throughout the world, where they recur at various times but never in the same form. This would suggest either a spontaneous origin based on similar observation, or similar processes, or a common origin with dissemination through oral or written transmission.

Riddles are found to exist on two levels: popular and learned, often passing from one group to the other. The Anglo-Saxon riddles illustrate both types of tendencies. While no positive distinction can be made between the two, in general the longer and more poetic ones, as also those containing runes, may safely be called learned; whereas, the shorter, and usually inferior ones, especially those dealing with simple domestic themes and the "obscene" riddles, must be regarded as popular. The transition from the popular to the learned, or literary form, is best exemplified by Riddle 84*.

As with similies and metaphors, riddles purport to represent something as something else. The significance of the resemblance, whether explicit or implicit, is assumed to be more or less easily recognised. Additionally, however, in the riddle, there is introduced an element of calculated deception; the resemblance is submerged in deliberate ambiguity or obscurity. Clues that are given are seldom obvious and the ambiguity tends to take one of two forms. In one, no deception

9

is intended beyond what would amount to a test of the hearer's mental agility in deducing the answer. In the other, the riddler sets out to trick the hearer maliciously, by forcing an ambiguity beyond the limits of fair play; or else possesses a special knowledge which his auditor cannot be expected to have. The one is an exercise of intelligence; the other a trial of wits, in which the riddler hopes to exhibit his superiority. The answers to the riddles are sometimes concealed in words, as in Riddle 13, or in signs, as in the runes. Riddle 45 indulges in a pun on the word **weax** and has two alternative solutions, one of which is obscene. When the riddle is versified, the ambiguity is heightened by the increment of poetical language. Or, as happens sometimes, the language is strained to satisfy metrical needs with the same result.

Aldhelm, Abbot of Malmesbury, and later, Bishop of Sherborne, is credited with the introduction of riddling into England. His prose work, **Epistola ad Acircium (695)**, included one hundred **Aenigmata** in hexameters, ranging in length from four to eighty-three lines on a great variety of subjects meant to glorify God's creation. They are, however, not riddles in the true sense in that they do not pose a problem and ask an answer, but are each headed by self-explanatory titles. Aldhelm drew his inspiration from the one hundred **Aenigmata** of Symphosius. Tatwine, Archbishop of Canterbury, and Eusebius, generally identified with Hwaethberht of Wearmouth and a friend of Bede, and Bede himself, all practised the art of riddling. Often such Latin riddles were exercises in metrical art merely; but many of them also provide much information on the daily life and customs of the time.

The earliest surviving riddle in Anglo-Saxon is a

10

free translation of one of Aldhelm's hundred **Aenigmata**, No.33 on the **lorica** or mail-coat, which exists in an eighth-century version in the Northumbrian dialect in a ninth-century copy in the University Library of Leiden. The Late West Saxon version of the same riddle appears in the Exeter Book, where it is No.35 among the first major group of riddles. The Northumbrian so-called Leiden Riddle could be early enough to be the work of Aldhelm; but, its Northumbrian, rather than West Saxon form, would seem to preclude this possibility. The Leiden Riddle, with its later version in the Exeter Book, looks back to the eighth century, and this may be assumed as about the time at which the practice of vernacular riddling began: it would seem to have continued almost up to the time when the Exeter Book in its present form was assembled at the close of the tenth century. This riddle, in which Aldhelm's elaborate lines on the **lorica** are simplified, retains much of the form that was to become typical of the Anglo-Saxon Riddles. The subject of the riddle, a coat of mail, speaks in its own person, describes its attributes - and what it is not - and then asks the listener to "say what this garment is." The **prosopopeia**, inherited from Latin usage, is common in the riddles, where it no doubt is employed in following the Latin models. This use of **prosopopeia**, by which a personified object is made to speak, is found in other Anglo-Saxon poems, notably **The Dream of the Rood**: and with this latter may be compared Riddles 30a* and 30b*, two versions of the same theme, which seem again to make the cross, its subject, speak personally.

There are two major groups of riddles in the Exeter Book numbered 1 to 59, and 61 to 95, separated in the manuscript by **The Wife's Lament**, a group of religious poems, **The Husband's Message**, and **The Ruin.** Riddle 60* concerns the inscription upon a piece of wood of a runic message between two intimates and precedes **The Husband's Message.** It is thus isolated from the main groups, unless one takes it as the introduction to **The Husband's Message,** as some have done.

The subjects, length, and treatment, of the riddles are varied. Natural phenomena are featured, such as tempest, winter, and ice; also weapons such as sword and bow, shield and ballista, and things from life in the hall such as the favourite honey drink, mead, and the harp. Then there are the marvels of God's creation, such as sun and moon, and birds like the cuckoo and the swan. There are themes from the varied aspects of the life of the time - a Bible codex, a weaver's loom, a garlic-seller. While most of these riddles are ingenious in the usual alliterative metre, occasionally there is true poetic power in dealing with Nature as in the Storm riddles. The most poetical instance of folklore is the Sun and Moon riddle.

Typical of these collections in general are the riddles of the swan and cuckoo, in which the well-known and traditional attributes of the birds are fancifully yet clearly set out in graceful short poems. In Riddle 14 the various uses of the horn, in peace and in war, for the mead-drinking in hall or at sea, are explained poetically, but with the echo of a very ancient folk-practice at the close. The listener is told in a formula as old as the Vedic hymns of the ancient Hindus, **"Fricge hwaet ic hatte:"** Ask what I am called.

A recognised feature of a riddle is that the solution might be difficult; or that it could be the deliberate setting of a puzzle to test ingenuity. Hence the use of runes and the making of a cryptogram. Riddle 23, to which the answer is a bow, Anglo-Saxon **boga**, gives its solution in its first word, spelled backward, with the **b** of **boga** replaced by **f** (a kind of interchange not unknown in early manuscripts). So the riddle begins: "Agof (boga) is my name." Riddle 47 is an illustration of a practice resorted to in the riddles of stating the answer to the problem in the opening line. It is one of the book-moth, and opens with the statement: "A moth ate words." Like several others in the Exeter Book collections of a more academic kind, this is a free adaptation from the Latin of Symphosius' **Aenigma**, No.16, **Tinea.**

While the normal metre is generally used in the riddles, all sorts of ingenious devices are to be met with, such as the use of onomatopoeia, as in Riddle 57, or of internal rhyme, as in Riddle 28. Although the poetry of these riddles cannot be considered to belong to the first class, it avails of the same poetic devices as the best Anglo-Saxon poems such as the "kenning," or descriptive periphrasis, and what is termed "parallel variation," or the repetition of different words, of the same thing or thought, in consecutive half-lines, often in a second half-line followed by a first.

The obscurity that is encountered in these poems is due partly to the fact that besides being intended to provide puzzles based on learned or popular ingenuity, we also lack the key to the knowledge of Anglo-Saxon life provided for their intended auditors or readers. Too often the text is corrupt, or apparently so; and especially, in the latter group of riddles, there are **lacunae** and evidence of casual or hasty copying.

There does not appear to be any orderly arrangement in this collection of riddles, as is to be expected, perhaps, of any collection. However, the Storm riddles are found together, as also those on birds (Riddles 7, 8, 9 and 10); whereas the six containing runes (Riddles 19, 24, 42, 58, 64 and 74) are scattered, and five of the seven "obscene" riddles (Riddles 25, 37, 44, 45 and 54) are among the first forty-nine, while the other two (Riddles 61 and 62) form a pair, like Riddles 44 and 45.

For the purpose of this edition, a tentative grouping coincident with certain broad categories has been attempted, despite the fact that a number of the solutions offered by scholars who have made the Riddles their particular subject of study are still in dispute.

The Exeter Book

The Exeter Book, chief of the four codices of Anglo-Saxon poetry, has belonged to the Chapter Library of Exeter Cathedral since 1072. It is listed in the catalogue of donations made to the Cathedral as "i mycel englisc boc gehwilcum þingum on leoþwisan geworht" by the Leofric who, in 1046, became Bishop of Devonshire and Cornwall. Written on vellum in a fine liturgical hand, the manuscript contains no drawings except a set of about sixty large initial letters. At some time the manuscript suffered considerable damage - the front had been used as a writing-board, and more appropriately as a beer-mat; an uncertain number of leaves at the beginning have been lost; and the last fourteen have been burnt through with a brand.

The manuscript is outstanding for the variety and range of its verse. Two of Cynewulf's signed poems are here, the Ascension, or Crist II, and Juliana, in addition to the Advent Lyrics, two poems on Judgment Day, the group of elegies that include The Wanderer and The Seafarer, part of an Anglo-Saxon Bestiary, or Physiologus,

describing the **Panther** and the **Whale,** the
Rhyming Poem, the **Phoenix,** one of the finest
religious poems written in Anglo-Saxon, and, of
course, the **Riddles.**

*These Riddles are not included in the present
selection.

THE

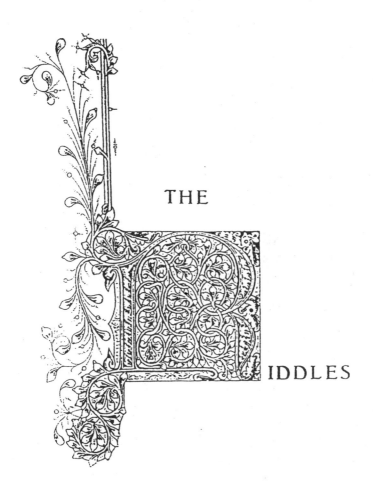

IDDLES

Hwylc is hæleþa   þæs horsc ꝫ þæs hygecræftig
þæt þæt mæge āsecgan,   hwā mec on sīð wræce?
Þonne ic āstīge   strong, stundum rēþe,
þrymful þunie,   þrāgum wræce
fēre geond foldan,   folcsalo bærne,
ræced rēafige,   rēcas stīgað
haswe ofer hrōfum,   hlin bið on eorþan,
wælcwealm wera.   Þonne ic wudu hrēre,
bearwas blēdhwate,   bēamas fylle
holme gehrēfed,   hea [h] um meahtum
wrecan on wāþe   wīde sended,
hæbbe mē on hrycge   þæt ær hādas wrēah
foldbūendra,   flæsc ꝫ gæstas
somod on sunde.   Saga hwā mec þecce,
oþþe hū ic hātte   þe þā hlæst bere.

NATURAL PHENOMENA

Riddle 1

HO IS THE MAN
so shrewd and sage
can say who sends me forth abroad,
when I rise strong, severely stern
with might resound, malicious move,
fare over land, the folk-halls fire,
houses spoil? Then smoke upsoars,
grey over roofs; riot rules on earth;
death-throes wrack men; I disturb the wood,
quick-growing grove, its trees lay low,
with water roofed, by potent powers
despatched to drive wide in my wandering.
I bear upon my back what erst enfolded forms
of earth-sojourners -flesh and spirits both
together- on the sea. Say who shelters me
or what my name is who that burden bears.

2.

Hwīlum ic gewīte,   swā ne wēnaþ men,
under ȳþa geþræc   eorþan sēcan,
garsecges grund.   Gifen biþ gewrēged,
. . . . ,   fām gewealcen;
·hwælmere hlimmeð,   hlūde grimmeð;
strēamas staþu bēatað,   stundum weorpaþ
on stealc hleoþa   stāne ꞇ sonde,
wāre ꞇ wǣge,   þonne ic winnende
holmmægne biþeaht   hrūsan styrge,
sīde sǣgrundas.   Sundhelme ne mæg
losian, ǣr mec lǣte,   sē þe mīn lāttēow bið
on sīþa gehwām.   Saga, þoncol mon,
hwā mec bregde   of brimes fæþmum
þonne strēamas eft   stille weorþað,
ȳþa geþwǣre,   þe mec ǣr wrugon.

Riddle 2

OMETIMES I SET OFF,
as men suppose not,
neath turbulent surges,
to seek out the earth,
the depths of the ocean. Disturbed is the main,
the foam upflung;
the whale-mere roars, loud rages then;
streams lash the shore, savagely cast
shingle and sand upon the steep slopes,
seaweed and wave, when struggling, I,
screened by sea-currents, the bottom stir up,
the vast ocean-deeps. Nor may the sea-surface
I scape ere the One who's my guide suffers me
on every excursion. Guess, erudite man,
who gathers me up from the grasp of the sea,
when the surges grow still again,
placid the waves, which covered me once.

Ic wiht geseah   wundorlīce
horn[um] bītwēonum   hūþe lǣdan,
lyftfæt lēohtlic   listum gegierwed,
hūþe to þām hām   of þām heresīþe;
walde hyre on þǣre byrig   būr ātimbra[n],
searwum āsettan,   gif hit swā meahte.
Ðā cwōm wundorlicu wiht   ofer wealles hrōf,
sēo is eallum cūð   eorðbūendum;
āhredde þā þā hūþe,   ┐ tō hām bedr[ā]f
wreccan ofer willan;   gewāt hyre west þonan
fǣhþum fēran,   forð ōnette.
Dust stonc tō heofonum;   dēaw fēol on eorþan;
niht forð gewāt.   Nǣnig siþþan
wera gewiste   þǣre wihte sīð.

Riddle 29

WIGHT IN WONDROUS
wise saw I
hale booty 'tween her horns,
a radiant air-vat, artfully adorned,
forage homewards from the fray;
she would a bower in that stronghold build herself,
with cunning it contrive, if so she could.
Then came a wondrous wight above the rampart's roof-
to all earth-dwellers is he known-
who snatched the spoil and homewards drove
the wanderer against her will. Thence went she west
faring from the fued, hastened forth.
Dust to the skies uprose; upon the ground fell dew;
night departed thence. Thereafter no
man wist where those wights journeyed to.

33.

Wiht cwōm æfter wēge   wrǣtlicu līþan,
cȳmlic from cēole   cleopode tō londe,
hlinsade hlūde ;   [h] leahtor wæs gryrelic,
egesful on earde,   ecge wǣron scearpe.
·Wæs hīo hetegrim,   hilde tō sǣne,
biter beadoweorca ;   bordweallas grōf
heard, hīþende;   heterūne bond.
Sægde searocræftig   ymb hyre sylfre gesceaft :
" Is mīn mōdor,   mæg [ð] a cynnes .
þæs dēorestan,   þæt is dohtor mīn,
ēacen ūp liden ;   swā þæt is ældum cūþ,
fīrum on folce,   þæt sēo on foldan sceal
on ealra londa gehwām   lissum stondan."

Riddle 33

ONDROUS CAME FLOATING
        a wight on the wave aft;
from the keel comely
        it called to the land,
loudly resounded;
        its laughter was grim,
on the earth fearful;
        its edges were sharp.
Hatefully cruel was it, in conflict quite sluggish,
in battle-deeds bitter; it stove in the shield-walls,
relentlessly ravaging. With baleful charms bound,
it cunningly discoursed of its own creation:
"My mother is of the kindred of maidens
the dearest, my daughter is she,
with travel grown gross, that is well-known of old
to me of the folk, that she shall upon earth
gloriously stand in lands everywhere."

Gewritu secgað   þæt sēo wiht sȳ
mid moncynne   miclum tī[d]um
sweotol ŋ gesȳne;   sundorcræft hafað
māra[n] micle   þonne hit men witen.
Hēo wile gesēcan   sundor æghwylcne
feorhberendra;   gewīteð eft fēran onweg;
ne bið hīo nǣfre   niht þǣr ōþre;
ac hīo sceal wīdeferh   wreccan lāste
hāmlēas hweorfan;   nō þȳ hēanre biþ.
Ne hafað hīo fōt ne folm,   ne ǣfre foldan hrān,
ne ēagen[a hafað]   ǣgþer twēga;
ne mūð hafaþ,   ne wiþ monnum spræc;
ne gewit hafað :   ac gewritu secgað
þæt sēo sȳ earmost   ealra wihta,
þāra þe æfter gecyndum   cenned wǣre.
Ne hafað hīo sāwle ne feorh;   ac hīo sīþas sceal
geond þās wundorworuld   wīde drēogan.
Ne hafaþ hīo blōd ne bān;   hwæþre bearnum wearð
geond þisne middangeard   mongum tō frōfre.
Nǣfre hīo heofonum hrān,   ne tō helle mōt;
ac hīo sceal wīdeferh   Wuldorcyninge[s]
lārum lifgan.   Long is tō secganne
hū hyre ealdorgesceaft   æfter gongeð,
wōh wyrda gesceapu.   þæt [is] wrǣtlic þing
tō gesecganne :   sōð is æghwylc
þāra þe ymb þās wiht   wordum bēcneð.
Ne hafað hē[o] ǣnig lim,   leofaþ efne sēþeah.
Gif þū mǣge rēselan   recene gesecgan
sōþum wordum,   saga hwæt hīo hātte.

Riddle 39

RITINGS SAY
this wight has been
for many years among mankind
clear and plain. A power it has
much more than men might comprehend.
It strives to seek each one apart
of those that live, then goes its way.
'Tis never there a second night,
but ever must the exile's track
rove homeless; none the humbler 'tis.
Neither foot nor hand has it, nor ever touches turf,
nor either of its eyes,
nor has it mouth, nor speaks with men,
nor has it wit; but writings say
that it is quite the basest of all beings
that after nature were begat.
Nor has it soul, nor life, but makes its way,
this wondrous world through, far and wide.
Neither blood nor bone has it; yet it becomes
to many men throughout this world an aid.
It never heaven touched, nor may it hell,
but it forever must by God's
injunctions live. Too long it is to tell
how its life-pattern later 'twill pursue,
fate's crooked ways; that is a wondrous thing
to chronicle. True then is each
word told about this wight;
nor has it any limb, yet nonetheless it lives.
If thou canst rede this riddle rapidly
with true words, say what it is called.

ONDROUS INTO THE WORLD'S
a warrior brought
by two mute beings for the use of men;
brightly extracted, which, for his hurt, bears
foe against foe. Oft strong though he be
a woman him binds; to them he bends well,
passively serves them, if him they attend,
maidens and men, in adequate measure
fairly him feed; he exalts them with favours
in life for their glee. He grimly requites
the one that allows him lofty to grow.

50.

Wiga is on eorþan   wundrum ācenned
dryhtum tō nytte   of dumbum twām,
torht ātyhted,   þone on tēon wigeð
fēond his fēonde.   F[o]rstrangne oft
wīf hine wrīð.   Hē him wel hēreð,
þēowaþ him geþwǣre,   gif him þegniað
mǣgeð ⁊ mǣcgas   mid gemete ryhte,
fēdað hine fǣgre;   hē him fremum stēpeð
līfe on lissum.   Lēanað grimme,
þe hine wloncne   weorþan lǣteð.

Riddle 6

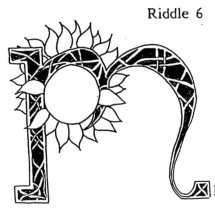

E, THE WIELDER
of victories, Christ,
for conflict created. Oft burn I the quick,
races unnumbered, ranged over the earth,
torment with trouble, though them I touch not,
whenever my master to battle bids me.
Sometimes the mood of the many I gladden;
sometimes I solace those I once assaulted
from very far off; they feel it, however,
the hurt and the healing, when afterwards I
favour their fortunes, despite deep affliction.

Mec gesette sōð   sigora Waldend,
Crīst, tō compe.   Oft ic cwice bærne,
unrīmu cyn   eorþan getenge,
næte mid nīþe,   swā ic him nō hrīne,
þon*ne* mec mīn Frēa   feohtan hāteþ.
Hwīlum ic monigra   mōd arēte;
hwīlum ic [wel] frēfre,   þā ic ær winne on
feorran swīþe :   hī þæs fēlað þēah,
swylce þæs ōþres,   þonne ic eft hyra
ofer dēop gedrēag   drohtað bēt[e].

11.

Hrægl is mīn hasofāg;⠀⠀hyrste beorhte,
rēade ⁊ scīre,⠀⠀on rēafe [hafu].
Ic dysge dwelle,⠀⠀⁊ dole hwette
[on]unrǣdsīþas;⠀⠀ōþrum stȳre
nyttre fōre. · Ic þæs nowiht wāt,
þæt hēo swā gemǣdde,⠀⠀mōde bestolene,
dǣde gedwolene, · dēoraþ mīne
wōn wīsan gehwām.⠀⠀Wā him þæs þēawes,
siþþan Hēah bringeð⠀⠀horda dēorast,
gif hī unrǣdes⠀⠀ǣr ne geswīcaþ.

30

GREY IS MY GARMENT;
                    ornaments bright,
            red and resplendent,
                        my raiment adorn.
The dull I misguide and the ignorant goad
to ventures imprudent; yet others prevent
from useful approaches; I wot not a whit
why they, maddened thus, bereft of their wits,
led astray in their deeds, should then applaud my
contrary ways. Woe to them for their conduct
when the Most High dispenses the dearest of gifts,
if they from their folly do not desist first.

43.

Ic wāt indryhtne,   æþelum dēorne
giest in geardum,   þām se grimma ne mæg
hungor sceððan   ne se hāta þurst,
yldo ne ādle.   Gif him ārlīce
esne þēnað,   sē ðe ā gān sceal
on þām sīðfate,   hȳ gesunde æt hām
findað, witode him,   wiste Ᵹ blisse,
cnōsles· unrīm ;   care, gif se esne
his hlāforde   hȳreð yfle,
frēan on fōre   Ne wile forht wesan
brōþor ōþrum ;   him þæt bām sceðeð,
þonne hȳ from bearme   bēgen hweorfað
ānre māgan   ellorfūse,
moddor Ᵹ sweostor.   Mon, sē þe wille,
·cȳþe cynewordum,   hū se cuma hātte
eðþa se esne,   þe ic hēr ymb sprice.

Riddle 43

NOBLE ONE I KNOW
that was nurtured
as a guest in that dwelling, who cannot by grim
hunger be harmed, nor yet by hot thirst,
nor old age, nor sickness. If him, as is seemly,
the servant attends, ever he who shall go
along on that journey, he safety at home
shall find him decreed, both food and delight,
and unnumbered kindred; but care, if the serf
obeys his lord badly,
his prince on the trip. Nor will they be timid
of each other, the brothers; that injures them both,
when they both together abandon the bosom
of their kindred quickly,
their mother and sister. Let whoever will,
in fitting words, set forth how that guest is called,
or the servant, about whom I speak at this time.

48.

Ic gefrægn f[o]r hæleþum   hring [ǣr]endean
torhtne būtan tungan,   tila, þēah hē hlūde
stefne ne cirmde   strongum wordum.
Sinc for secgum   swīgende cwæð :
" Gehǣle mec, · Helpend gǣsta ! "
Rȳne ongietan   rēadan goldes
guman, galdorcwide;   glēawe beþuncan
hyra hǣlo tō Gode,   swā se hring gecwæð.

HEARD A RING
                    for heroes plead,
beautiful, tongueless, well, though with loud
voice it cried not; strong words it wove.
This treasure of men silently spoke:
"Healer of souls, do Thou heal me!"
May the rune of the red gold men understand,
its magic import; may the prudent entrust
their redemption to God just as the ring said.

55.

Ic seah in heall,   þǣr hæleð druncon,
on flet beran   fēower cynna :
wrǣtlic wudutrēow   ⁊ wunden gold,
sinc searobunden,   ⁊ seolfres dǣl
⁊ rōde tācn,   þæs ūs tō roderum ūp
hlǣdre rǣrde,   ǣr hē helwara
burg ābrǣce.   Ic þæs bēames mæg
ēaþe for eorlum   æþelu secgan :
þǣr wæs hlin ⁊ ā[c]   ⁊ se hearda īw
⁊ se fealwa holen.   Frēan sindon ealle
nyt ætgædre;   naman habbað ānne,
wulfhēafedtrēo,   þæt oft wǣpen ābæd
his mondryhtne,   māðm in healle,
goldhilted sweord.   Nū mē [gieddes þisses]
ondsware ȳwe,   sē hine onmēde
wordum secgan,   hū se wudu hātte.

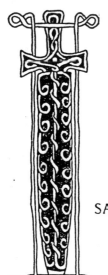

Riddle 55

SAW IN THE HALL,
     where heroes were drinking,
     borne onto the floor,
          a thing of four kinds,
     a wonderful wood-tree,
          with gold that was twisted,
a subtly-bound treasure, silver in part,
and a rood-symbol which
for us to the heavens
a ladder erected, ere the people of hell's
castle he stormed. I can of that wood's
excellence easily speak before men;
maple and oak were there and the tough yew
and the dark holly; they are to the lord
all together of help; one name have they:
Wolf-head Tree. Oft that afforded a weapon
its lord, in the hall a precious heirloom,
a gold-hilted sword. To me now this riddle's
answer reveal; himself he requites
who, with words, can declare what that wood is called.

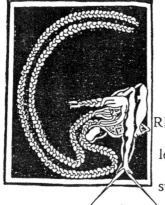

GREATER AM I
    than this world is,
  lesser than the handworm,
    lighter than the moon,
  swifter than the sun.
          All the seas and
floods are in my grasp, and the bosom of earth,
and the green plains. I probe the depths,
descend below hell, rise over the heavens,
the region of glory; amply I reach
above the angels' abode, pervade the earth,
the whole world and the ocean-streams
widely with myself. Say what I'm called.

Ic eom māre   þonne þes mi[d]dangeard,
læsse þonne hondwyrm,   lēohtre þonne mōna,
swiftre þonne sunne.   Sæs mē sind ealle,
flōdas, on fæðmum   ʒ þ[ē]s foldan bearm,
grēne wongas.   Grundum ic hrīne,
helle underhnīge;   heofonas oferstīge,
wuldres ēþel,   wīde ræce
ofer engla eard;   eorþan gefylle,
ea[l]ne middangeard   ʒ merestrēamas
sīde, mid mē sylfum.   Saga hwæt ic hātte.

BIRDS

Riddle 7

USHED IS MY GARB,
      when I tread on the ground,
or sojourn in creeks, or the shallows stir up.
Over men's homes there heave me sometimes
my trappings, and this tulmultous wind,
and widely the might of the welkin me then
bears over mankind. These adornments of mine
loudly resound and melody make;
lustily sing, when I am not lying
on flood and on field - a wayfaring sprite.

Hrægl mīn swīgað,   þonne ic hrūsan trede
oþþe þā wīc būge   oþþe wado drēfe.
Hwīlum mec āhebbað   ofer hæleþa byht
hyrste mīne   ꞇ þēos hēa lyft,
ꞇ mec þonne wīde   wolcna strengu
ofer folc byreð;   frætwe mīne
swōgað hlūde   ꞇ swinsiað,
torhte singað,   þonne ic getenge ne bēom
flōde ꞇ foldan,   fērende gǣst.

39

8.

Ic þurh mūþ sprece   mongum reordum,
wrencum singe,   wrixle geneahhe
hēafodwōþe,   hlūde cirme,
healde mīne wīsan,   hlēoþre ne mīþe.
Eald æfensceop,   eorlum bringe
blisse in burgum ;   þonne ic būgendre
stefne styrme,   stille on wīcum
sit [ta] ð [h] nīgende.   Saga hwæt ic hātte,
þ[e] swā scīre [c]īge,   scēawendwīsan
hlūde onhyrge,   hæleþum bodige
wilcumena fela   wōþe mīnre.

Riddle 8

HROUGH MY MOUTH I SPEAK
                         with many tongues;
with modulating chant, I often change
my voice; I cry aloud,
my manner hold, not hide the melody.
Old evening bard, to men I bring
bliss in towns, when I transform
my tone to sing out; still at home
they silent sit. Say what I'm called,
who, brightly thus, buffoons
do imitate aloud, to men announce
with my voice many welcome things.

9.

Mec on þissum dagum   dēadne ofgēafu[n]
fæder ꝥ mōdor;   ne wæs mē feorh þā gēn,
ealdor in innan. ·þā mec [ān] ongon
wel hold mē   gewēdum [þ]eccan,
hēold ꝥ freoþode,   hlēosceorpe wrāh
s[w]ē ārlīce   swā hire āgen bearn,
oþþæt ic under scēate,   swā mīn gesceapu wǣron,
ungesibbum wearð   ēacen gǣste.
Mec sēo friþemǣg   fēdde siþþan,
ˌoþþæt ic āwēox,   wīddor meahte
sīþas āsettan;   hēo hæfde swǣsra þȳ lǣs
suna ꝥ dohtra,   þȳ hēo swā dyde.

42

Riddle 9

I
N THOSE DAYS
            they abandoned me for dead,
father and mother both; nor yet in me was life
or stir within. Then someone tried
to cover me with clothes, a woman kind;
watched and cherished, wrapped me in a robe
as gently as she would her proper progeny,
until beneath her breast, as was my destiny,
I grew, a stranger, strong amid those not
my kin. That tender fostress fed me afterwards
till I waxed sound, more widely could
set forth on trips; the fewer of her own had she,
dear sons and daughters, due to what she did.

13.

Ic seah turf tredan;   X wǣron ealra,
VI gebrōþor   ⁊ hyra sweostor mid;
hæfdon feorg cwico.   Fell hongedon
sweotol ⁊ gesȳne   on seleᶊ wǣge
ānra gehwylces.   Ne wæs hyra ængum þȳ wyrs,
ne sīde þȳ sārre,   þēah hȳ swā sceoldon
rēafe bīrofene,   rodra Weardes
meahtum āweahte,   mūþum slītan
haswe blēde.   Hrægl biꝺ genīwad
þām þe ǣr forꝺcymene   frætwe lēton
licgan on lāste,   gewitan lond tredan.

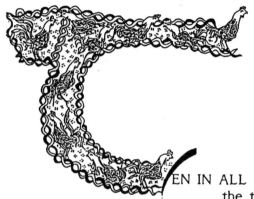

EN IN ALL
                        the turf saw I tread,
brothers six and their sisters too;
beings that were live. Their skins hung from
their house-wall, clear and manifest,
every one. Nor were any of them the worse,
nor their going the sorer, though they should thus,
bereft of their raiment, by the firmaments' Lord's
might aroused, rend with their mouths
the grey-green shoots. Their garment's renewed
who before birth their accoutrements leave
behind them to lie when they tread upon land.

57.

Ðēos lyft byreð   lȳtle wihte
ofer beorghleoþa,   þā sind blace swīþe,
swearte, salopāde.   Sanges rō[f]e
hēapum fērað,   hlūde cirmað;
tredað bearonæssas,   hwīlum burgsalo
niþþa bearna.   Nemnað hȳ sylfe.

MALL SPRITES
                    this wind sustains
          over the hillsides.
                    Quite bright are they,
black and dark-coated. Doughty of song,
they fare in flocks; loudly they cry;
the headlands they tread, sometimes the houses
of the children of men. They name themselves.

12.

Fōtum ic fēre,   foldan slīte,
grēne wongas,   þenden ic gǣst bere.
Gif mē feorh losað,   fæste binde
swearte Wēalas,   hwīlum sēllan men.
Hwīlum ic dēorum   drincan selle
beorn [e] of bōsme;   hwīlum mec brȳd triedeð
felawlonc fōtum.   Hwīlum feorran brōht,
wonfeax Wāle   wegeð ⁊ þȳð,
dol druncmennen,   deorcum nihtum,
·wǣteð in wætre,   wyrmeð hwīlum
fǣgre tō fȳre;   mē on fæðme sticaþ
hygegālan hond;   hwyrfeð geneahhe,
swīfeð mē geond sweartne.   Saga hwæt ic hātte,
þe ic lifgende   lond rēafige,
⁊ æfter dēaþe   dryhtum þēowige.

ANIMALS

Riddle 12

FARE ON FEET,
                    the turf tear up,
        the green plains,
                    while I spirit bear.
        If I lose life, I bind secure
the swart Welsh, sometimes better men.
Drink I sometimes give a bold
man from my bosom; me, at times, a bride treads
proudly underfoot; fetched from afar, at times,
the dark-haired slave conveys and squeezes me;
the foolish drunken servant maid on darksome nights,
in water wets me, sometimes warms
me fair beside the fire; into my bosom thrusts
her wanton hands, revolves them frequently,
sweeps me in the dark. Say what I'm called,
who, living, ravage land
and, after death, administer to men.

49

15.

Hals is mīn hwīt   ⁊ hēafod fealo,
sīdan swā some;   swift ic ēom on fēþe;
beadowǣpen bere;   mē on bæce standa ð hēr,
swylce suē on [h]lēorum;   hlīfiað tū
ēaran ofer ēagum;   ordum ic steppe
in grēne græs.   Mē bið gyrn witod,
gif mec onhǣle   ān onfindeð
wælgrim wiga,   þǣr ic wīc būge,
b[ol]d mid bearnum;   ⁊ ic bīde þǣr
mid geoguðcnōsle,   hwonne gæst cume
tō durum mīnum.   Him biþ dēað witod;
forþon ic sceal of ēðle   eaforan mīne
forhtmōd fergan,   flēame nergan:
gif hē mē æfterweard   ealles weorþeð,
hine berað brēost.   Ic his bīdan ne dear
rēþes on gerūman   (nele þæt rǣd teal[a]),
ac ic sceal fromlīce   fēþemundum
þurh stēapne beorg   strǣte wyrcan.
Ēaþe ic mæg frēora   feorh genergan,
gif ic mǣgburge mōt   mīne gelǣdan
on dēgolne weg   þurh dū[ne] þȳrel
swǣse ⁊ gesibbe;   ic mē siþþan ne þearf
wælhwelpes wīg   wiht onsittan.
Gif [s]e nīðsceaþa   nearwe stīge
mē on swaþe sēceþ,   ne tōsǣleþ him
on þām gegnpaþe   guþgemōtes,
siþþan ic þurh hylles   hrōf gerǣce
⁊ þurh hēst hrīno   hildepīlum
lāðgewinnum,   þām þe ic longe flēah.

Riddle 15

HITE IS MY NECK
and tawny my head,
so too are my sides. Swift in motion am I
who bears battle-gear. Upon my back stand
hairs such as those on my cheeks. Tower two
ears over my eyes. I tread on my toes
in the green grass. For me is there grief
if anyone within my covert catch me,
a warrior grim, where I hide in my haunt,
my lair with my litter; and there do I lurk
with my incipient brood when the intruder comes
up to my doors; for them death is doomed.
So must my offspring I from our abode
faint-hearted bear, protect them by flight,
if he should come following close after me;
a-crawl on his breast. I dare not abide his
fierce deeds in my den -that were ill-counsel-
but then must I fast with my forefeet
a passage provide through the high hill.
I can easily save the lives of my loved ones
if I be allowed my household to lead
by a hidden route through a hole in the hill,
my kinsfolk and dear ones; later I need not
a whit the encounter dread with the death-whelp.
If the savage adversary along a straight path
pursues me behind, he shall surely not lack
the conflict of battle on his hostile course
when I reach through the roof of the hill
and with war-darts strike wildly
the malignant foe from whom I long fled.

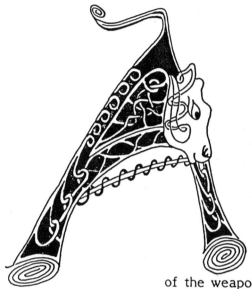

WIGHT
of the weaponed kind saw I
greedy of youthful joys; a gift he gave
of four life-saving springs
to shoot forth brightly, gush in fitting form.
A man spoke, who declared to me:
"This wight, if he survive, will break the downs;
if burst asunder, will the living bind."

Ic þā wiht geseah   wǣpnedcynnes
geoguðmyrwe grǣdig.   Him on gafol forlēt
Ferðfriþende   fēower wellan
scīre scēotan,   on gesceap þēotan.
Mon maþelade,   sē þe mē gesægde:
"Sēo wiht, gif hīo gedȳgeð,   dūna briceð;
gif hē tōbirsteð,   bindeð cwice."

Riddle 4

Y THANE MUST I BUSY
from time to time,
ring-bound, readily obey,
destroy my rest, and noisily declare
my master gave me a band for my neck.
Me oft the sleep-weary maiden or man
hastes to greet; hostile towards him I
wintry-cold answer: "A warm limb
the bound ring bursts sometimes!"
However, 'tis sportive unto my servant,
a half-witted man, to me likewise,
when one knows aught and so with words
my riddle can rightly give answer to.

Ic sceal þrāgbysig   þegne mīnum
hringan hæfted   hȳran georne,
mīn bed brecan,   breahtme cȳþan
þæt mē halswriþan   hlāford sealde.
Oft mec slæpwērigne   secg oðþe mēowle
grētan ēode;   ic him gromheortum
winterceald oncweþe :   "Wearm lim
gebundenne b[ēa]g   [bersteð hwīlum]."
Sēþēah biþ on þonce   þegne mīnum,
medwīsum men,   mē þæt sylfe,
þær wiht wite,   ꞇ wordum mīn
on spēd mæge   spel gesecgan.

21

Neb is mīn niþerweard;   nēol ic fēre
ꝥ be grunde græfe,   geonge swā mē wīsað
hār holtes fēond;   ꝥ hlāford mīn
[on] wōh færeð,   weard, æt steorte,
wrīgaþ on wonge,   wegeð mec ꝥ þȳð,
sāweþ on swæð mīn.   Ic snyþige forð
brungen of bear[w]e,   bunden cræfte,
wegen on wægne;   hæbbe wundra fela.
Mē biþ gongendre   grēne on healfe,
ꝥ mīn swæð sweotol   sweart on ōþre.
Mē þurh hrycg wrecen   hongaþ under
ān orþonc pīl,   ōþer on hēafde
fæst ꝥ forðweard   fealleþ on sīdan,
ꝥæt ic tōþum tere,   gif mē teala þēnaþ
hindeweardre   þæt biþ hlāford mīn.

Riddle 21

Y NOSE INCLINES
downward; deeply I fare
and dig up the ground; I move as he guides me,
the grey foe of the forest and my overseer,
who double-bent goes, the guide at my tail.
He drives, urges, presses me into the plain,
sows in my swath. I go sniffing the ground,
brought from the grove, bound strong,
borne on the wain. Many wounds have I;
on one side of me, as I go, there is green;
and, on the other, my swath is clear swart.
Through my back driven, there hangs underneath
an ingenious point, on my head yet another;
fixed and prone. At the side falls
what I tear with my teeth, if rightly he serves me
from behind, who my master is.

I SAW A WIGHT,
in the dwellings of men,
that feeds the cattle.
It has many teeth;
the beak is gainful,
downward it goes,
ravages faithfully and then returns home;
wanders along walls, reaches for roots;
always it finds those that are not firm;
the fair ones it leaves fixed by their roots
in their station still standing,
brightly gleaming, blooming and growing.

Ic wiht geseah   in wera burgum
sēo þæt feoh fēdeð;   hafað fela tōþa;
nebb biþ hyre æt nytte;   niþerweard gongeð,
hīþeð holdlīce   ꝺ tō hām tȳhð,
wǣþeð geond weallas,   wyrte sēceð.
Āā hēo þā findeð   þā þe fæst ne biþ;
lǣteð hīo þā wlitigan,   wyrtum fæste,
stille stondan   on staþolwonge,
beorhte blīcan,   blōwan ꝺ grōwan.

Riddle 49

NE I KNOW STANDS SETTLED,
deaf and dumb, who,
oft by day, devours
gifts greedily, the slave's hand from.
Sometimes in the dwellings the dark-hued thane,
dusky and dun-faced, despatches others
down its gullet, dearer than gold,
which the noble-born desire oft,
kings and queens. Its nature yet now
I will name not, who to them is thus of use,
and does good, what the dumb one here,
the swarthy nitwit, swallows first.

Ic wāt eardfæstne   ānne standan
dēafne dumban,   sē oft dæges swilgeð
þurh gōpes hond   gifrum lācum.
Hwīlu[m] on þām wīcum   se wonna þegn,
sweart ᛣ saloneb,   sendeð ōþre
under gōman him   golde dȳrran,
þā æþelingas   oft wilniað,
cyningas ᛣ cwēne.   Ic þæt cyn nū gēn
nemnan ne wille,   þe him to nytte swā
ᛣ to dugþum dōþ,   þæt se dumba hēr,
eorp unwita,   ǣr f[o]rswilgeð.

56.

Ic wæs þærinne,   þær ic āne geseah
winnende wiht   wido bennegean,
holt hweorfende;   heaþoglemma fēng,
dēopra dolga.   Daroþas wǣron
wē[a] þǣre wihte,   ⁊ se wudu searwum
fæste gebunden.   Hyre fōta wæs
biidfæst ōþer;   ōþer bisgo drēag,
leolc on lyfte,   hwīlum londe nēah.
Trēow wæs [þām] getenge,   þe þǣr torhtan stōd
lēafum bīhongen.   Ic lāfe geseah
mīnum hlāforde,   þǣr hæleð druncon,
þāra flān[geweorca]   on flet beran.

Riddle 56

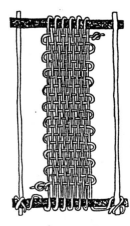 WAS IN THERE
when I something saw:
wood wound a struggling wight,
the moving beam; battle-hurts it took,
deep scars. Spears were
that wight's woe, and cunningly the wood
was fast bound. One of its feet was
fixed; the other laboured busily,
played aloft, nigh the land sometimes.
Nearby was a tree that brightly stood
with leaves adorned. I saw the rest
for my lord, where warriors drank,
of arrow-work, borne to the hall.

58.

Ic wāt ānfēte   ellen drēogan
wiht on wonge.   Wīde ne fēreð,
ne fela rīdeð,   ne flēogan mæg
þurh scīrne dæg,   ne hīe scip fereð,
naca nægledbord;   nyt bið hwæþre
hyre [mon]dryhtne   monegum tīdum.
Hafað hefigne steort,   hēafod lȳtel,
tungan lange,   tōð nænigne,
īsernes dæl;   eorðgræf pæþeð.
Wætan ne swelgeþ,   ne wiht iteþ,
fōþres ne gītsað,   fereð oft swāþēah
lagoflōd on lyfte;   līfe ne gielpeð,
hlāfordes gifum,   hȳreð swāþēana
þēodne sīnum.   þrȳ sind in naman
ryhte rūnstafas;   þāra is Rād f[o]r[ma].

Riddle 58

"ONE-FOOTED" WIGHT
I know to work
with fortitude in the fields. It fares not far,
nor rides much; nor can it fly
during the bright day, nor does it bark,
a boat with nailed boards, bear it; yet
it is often of use to its lord.
It has a heavy tail, a tiny head,
a long tongue, no tooth.
Of iron, in part, it treads the pit.
Nor swallows liquid, nor eats aught,
it craves not food; yet oft it conveys
water aloft. It brags not of life,
of the lord's gifts; nonetheless, it obeys
its master. In its name there are three
real runes of which RAD is the first.

61

65.

Cwico wæs ic, ne cwæð ic wiht;   cwele ic efne sēþēah.
Ær ic wæs, eft ic cwōm.   Æghwā mec rēafað,
hafað mec on hea[ð]re   ꝥ mīn hēafod scireþ,
bīteð mec on bær līc,   briceð mīne wisan.
·Monnan ic ne bīte,   nym[þ]e hē mē bīte;
sindan þāra monige   þe mec bītað..

LIVE I WAS, BUT I SAID NAUGHT;
even so I die.
Ere I had been, back I returned. Everybody reaves me,
keeps me confined, and shears off my head,
my bare body bites, breaks my sprouts.
I bite no man, save he bites me;
many there are who do bite me.

Mīn hēafod is   homere geþuren,
searopīla wund,   sworfen fēole.
Oft ic begīne   þæt mē ongean sticað,
þonne ic hnītan sceal   hringum gyrded
hearde wið heardum,   hindan þȳrel
forð āscūfan   þæt [frēan mīnes]
mōd - · ᚹ · freoþað   middelnihtum.
Hwīlum ic under bæc   bregde nebbe,
hyrde þæs hordes,   þonne mīn hlāford wile
·lāfe þicgan,   þāra þe hē of līfe hēt
wælcræf[te] āwrecan,   willum sīnum.

Y HEAD IS
with a hammer forged,
with sharp tools wounded, smoothed with files.
I often stare at what is stuck before me,
when girt with rings, I must needs thrust
hard against hard; pierced from behind,
I forward shove that which my lord's
mind holds the midnight pleasure of.
My beak I sometimes backwards draw
when the hoard's herd, my lord, desires,
their leavings to keep whom he ordered from life
to be driven, at his will, by battle-craft.

26.

Mec fēonda sum   fēore besnyþede,
woruldstrenga bīnō*m*,   wǣtte siþþan,
dȳfde on wætre,   · dyde eft þonan,
sette on sunnàn,   þǣr ic swīþe belēas
hērum þām þe ic hæfde.   Heard mec siþþan
snāð seaxes ecg   sindrum begrunden,
fingras fēoldan;   7 mec fugles wyn
geond spēddropum   spyrede geneahhe
ofer brūnne brerd,   bēamtelge swealg,
strēames dǣle,   stōp eft on mec,
sīþade sweartlāst.   Mec siþþan wrāh?
hæleð hlēobordum,   hȳ[d]e beþenede,
gierede mec mid golde;   forþon mē glīwedon
wrǣtlic weorc smiþa   wīre bīfongen.
Nū þā gerēno   7 se rēada telg
7 þā wuldorgesteald   wīde mǣre[n]
dryhtfolca Helm!   nales dol wīte!
Gif mīn bearn wera   brūcan willað,
hȳ bēoð þȳ gesundran   7 þȳ sigefæstran,
heortum þȳ hwætran,   7 þȳ hygeblīþran,
ferþe þȳ frōdran;   habbaþ frēonda þȳ mā
swǣsra 7 gesibbra,   sōþra 7 gōdra,
tilra 7 getrēowra,   þā hyra tȳr 7 ēad

ēstum ȳcað,   7 hȳ ārstafum,
lissum, bīlecgað,   7 hī lufan fæþmum
fæste clyppað.   Frige hwæt ic hātte,
niþum to nytte.   Nama mīn is mǣre,
hæleþum gifre,   7 hālig sylf.

WRITING

Riddle 26

A CERTAIN FOE REFT ME
                                          of life,
   deprived me of my worldly strength,
                              then moistened me,
 dipped me in water, later took me thence,
set me in the sun where I soon lost
the hairs I had. Then me the hard
knife's edge cut, ground away the dross;
fingers folded me, and the fowl's delight
throughout with drops made tracks abundantly,
across the brown brim, absorbed the tree-dye,
a part of the stream, on me stopped again,
dark brown traces left. Then, me enwrapped,
with boards, a man, spread skin across,
with gold geared me; so beautified me
the wondrous work of smiths, with wire engirt.
Now the embellishments and the red dye
and the precious possessions make famous afar
the Guardian of Nations, not the pains of conceit.
If the children of men are willing to use me,
the sounder will they be and surer of triumph,
the bolder in heart, and the blither in thought.
The wiser in life, the more friends will they have,
dearer and closer, truer and better,
nobler and stauncher, who their glory and wealth
will gladly increase; and, with goodness
and kindness surround them; and, with loving embraces
close clasp them. Ask what I am called,
useful to men. My name is renowned,
salvation to heroes, and sacred myself.

MOTH DEVOURED WORDS.
That seemed to me
a fate remarkable, when of
that marvel I was told,
that the worm, a warrior's song had swallowed up,
a felon in the dark, the famous utterance
and its strong place. The pilfering stranger was
no whit the wiser, though he ate the words.

Moððe word fræt.   Mē þæt þūhte
wrǣtlicu wyrd,   þā ic þæt wundor gefrægn,
þæt se wyrm forswealg   wera gied sumes,
þēof in þȳstro   þrymfæstne cwide
⁊ þæs strangan staþol.   Stælgiest ne wæs
wihte þȳ glēawra,   þē hē þām wordum swealg.

Riddle 51

SAW FOUR CREATURES
splendidly
travel together; black were their tracks,
their marks quite swart. Swift was its course
as of fast fowl; it flew through the air,
dived under the wave. Unceasing, laboured
the struggling warrior who shows them the way,
all of the four over the plated gold.

Ic seah wrǣtlice   wuhte fēower
samed sīþian;   swearte wǣran lāstas,
swaþu swīþe blacu.   Swift wæs on fōre,
fuglum fr[o]mra   flēotgan lyfte;
dēaf under ȳþe.   Drēag unstille,
winnende wiga,   sē him w[e]gas tǣcneþ
ofer fǣted gold   fēower eallum.

Is þes middangeard   missenlicum
wīsum gewlitegad,   wrǣttum gefrætwad.
Ic seah sellic þing   singan on ræcede;
wiht wæs [nōwēr]   werum on gemonge
sīo hæfde wæstum   wundorlicran.
Niþerwear[d]   wæs neb hyre,
fēt ˥ folme   fugele gelīce;
nō hwæþre flēogan mæg,   ne fela gongan.
Hwæþre fēþegeorn   fremman onginneð
gecoren cræftum,   cyrreð geneahhe
oft ˥ gelōme   eorlum on gemonge,
siteð æt symble,   sǣles bīdeþ,
hwonne ǣr hēo cræft   hyre cȳþan mōte
werum on wonge.   Ne hēo þǣr wiht þigeð
þæs þe him æt blisse   beornas habba[ð].
Dēor, dōmes georn,   hīo dumb wunað;
hwæþre hyre is on fōte   fǣger hlēoþor,
wynlicu wōðgiefu;   wrǣtlic mē þinceð
hū sēo wiht mæge   wordum lācan
þurh fōt neoþan   frætwed hyrstum.
Hafað hyre on halse,   þonne hīo hord warað,
bær, bēagum deall,   brōþor sīne,
mæg mid mǣg[um].   Micel is tō hycgenne
wīsum wōðboran,   hwæt [sīo] wiht sīe.

MUSIC

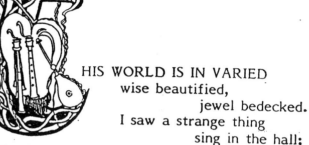

HIS WORLD IS IN VARIED
    wise beautified,
            jewel bedecked.
   I saw a strange thing
          sing in the hall;
in nature, among men, was naught to compare,
for a most curious form it had.
Its beak inclined downwards,
bird-like its feet and hands;
yet, it cannot fly, nor wander at will.
Still eager for movement, it starts to advance,
with chosen craft; it frequently turns,
again and again, among men
who sit at the banquet-board, bides its time
till it can reveal its craft before
men who are nigh. It partakes of naught
that the men that are there possess for their glee.
Dauntless, eager for glory, dumb it remains;
yet, in its foot, it has a fair melody,
glorious song-gift. Wondrous methinks
how this wight can with words play
through its foot underneath, with trappings adorned.
It holds on its neck, as it guards its hoard,
bare resplendent with rings, its brothers two,
kinsmen strong. Great 'tis to think,
for a wise singer, what this wight be.

Wiht is wrǣtlic   þām þe hyr[e] wīsan ne conn:
singeð þurh sīdan ;   is se swēora wōh
orþoncum geworht ;   hafaþ eaxle t[w]ā
scearp on gescyldrum.   His gesceapo [drēogeð],
.þe swā wrǣtlīce   be wege stonde
hēah ꝺ hlēortorht   hæleþum tō nytte.

ONDROUS THAT WIGHT IS
when its ways are not known.
It sings through its sides. Curved is its neck,
cunningly wrought; two shoulders it has,
sharp on its spine. It follows its fate
when it stands by the way, wondrously so,
high and bright-hued, of profit to men.

5.

Ic eom ānhaga   īserne wund,
bille gebennad,   beadoweorca sæd,
ecgum wērig.   Oft ic wīg sēo,
frecne feohtan ;   frōfre ne wēne,
þæt mē gēoc cyme   gūðgewinnes,
ǣr ic mid ældum   eal forwurde ;
ac mec hnossiað   homera lāfe
heardecg, heoroscearp,   hondweorc smiþa
bītað in burgum ;   ic ā bīdan sceal
lāþran gemōtes.   Nǣfre lǣcecynn
on folcstede   findan meahte,
þāra þe mid wyrtum   wunde gehǣlde ;
ac mē ecga dolg   ēacen weorðað
þurh dēaðslege   dagum ꝫ nihtum.

Riddle 5

 LONE-STEPPER I,
wounded with steel,
stricken with sword, sated with battle-work,
weary of blades. Oft I behold war,
a wicked foe fight. I look not for comfort,
that out of the struggle come safety to me,
ere among heroes I perish utterly;
but the hammered blades smite me;
the hard-edged sharp swords, the skilled craft of smiths,
bite in the citadels; I must abide
a more hostile encounter. Not one of the leech-kind
could I find in the city
of those who with herbs healed hurts,
but my sword-scars grew greater
with death blows by day and night.

17.

Ic eom mundbora   mīnre heorde,
eodorwīrum fæst,   innan gefylled
dryhtgestrēona.   Dægtīdum oft
spǣte sperebrōgan ;   spēd biþ þȳ māre
fylle mīnre ;   frē[a] þæt bīhealdeð,
hū mē of hrife flēogað   hyldepīlas.
Hwīlum ic sweartum   swelgan onginne
brūnum beadowǣpnum,   bitrum ordum,
eglum attorsperum.   Is mīn innað til,
wombhord wlitig,   wloncum deore.
Men gemunan   þæt mē þurh mūþ fareð.

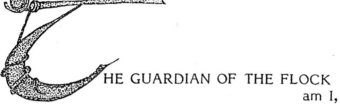

HE GUARDIAN OF THE FLOCK
am I,
with wires fast engirt and filled within
with lordly wealth. By day most oft
spear-dread I spit abroad; success is the greater
for my surfeit. The master this beholds,
how the war-darts from my womb emerge.
Sometimes I swallow swart
brown battle-gear, bitter points,
deadly poisoned darts. My innards are of use,
my womb-hoard pretty, precious to proud warriors;
men remember what fares through my mouth.

23.

Agof is mīn noma   eft onhwyrfed.
Ic eom wrǣtlic wiht   on gewin sceapen.
Þonne ic onbūge,   ⁊ me of bōsme fareð
ǣtren onga,   ic bēom eallgearo
þæt ic mē þæt feorhbealo   feor āswāpe.
Siþþan mē se waldend,   sē mē þæt wīte gescōp,
leoþo forlǣteð,   ic bēo lengre þonne ǣr,
oþþæt ic spǣte   spilde geblonden,
ealfelo attor,   þæt ic ǣr gēap.
Ne tōgongeð þæs   gumena hwylcum
ǣnigum ēaþe,   þæt ic þǣr ymb sprice,
gif hine hrīneð   þæt mē of hrife flēogeð,
þæt þone māndrinc   mægne gecēapaþ,
full wer fæste   fēore sīne.
Nelle ic unbunden   ǣnigum hȳran,
nymþe searosǣlod.   Saga hwæt ic hātte.

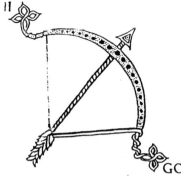

"GOF" IS MY NAME REVERSED;
a wondrous wight am I, in struggle shaped.
When I bend and from my bosom fares
the poisoned dart, I am disposed
to fling that deadly evil far from me.
When the master who designs that misery for me,
my limbs releases, I am no longer than before,
until with ruin blent, I retch
the baleful bane I swallowed earlier.
It leaves no man,
not any, lightly, that of which I speak;
if that which flees my womb touch him,
that deadly drink he pays for with his strength,
a full atonement firmly with his life.
When unstrung, I list to none,
unless bound cunningly. Say what I'm called.

35.

Mec se wǣta wong   wundrum frēorig
of his innaþe   ǣrist cende.
Ne wāt ic mec beworhtne   wulle flȳsum,
hǣrum þurh hēahcrǣft,   hygeþoncum mīn.
Wundene mē ne bēoð wefle,   ne ic wearp hafu,
ne þurh þrēata geþrǣcu   þrǣd mē ne hlimmeð,
ne æt mē hrūtende   hrīsil scrīþeð,
ne᾿ mec ōhwonan sceal   āmas cnyssan.
Wyrmas mec ne āwǣfan   wyrda crǣftum,
þā þe geolo godwebb   geatwum frætwað.
Wile mec mon hwæþre sēþēah   wīde ofer eorþan
hātan for hæleþum   hyhtlic gewǣde.
Saga, sōðcwidum,   searoþoncum glēaw,
wordum wīsfæst,   hwæt þis gewǣd[e] sȳ.

E THE WET EARTH,
wondrous frore,
first brought forth
from the womb.
I am not wrought of the fleece of wool
or of hairs with high skill; that I know in my mind.
Woofs are not wound round me, nor have I warp,
nor through the threat of force does thread
of mine resound,
nor whirring shuttle move across me on any side.
Worms move me not with fatal wiles
which fairly adorn the fine yellow web.
Yet widely over the world will they
call me the glad garment of heroes.
Tell me in true speech, o thou skilled in sagacity,
wise in words, what this dress may be.

14.

Ic wæs wǣpenwiga;   nū mec wlonc þeceð
geong hagostealdmon   golde ꝺ sylfore,
wōum wīrbogum.   Hwīlum weras cyssað;
hwīlum ic tō hilde   hlēoþre bonne
wilgehlēþan;   hwīlum ,wycg byreþ
mec ofer mearce,   hwīlum merehengest
fereð ofer flōdas   frætwum beorhtne;
hwīlum mægða sum   mīnne gefylleð
bōsm bēaghroden;   hwīlum ic bordum sceal,
heard, hēafodlēas,   behlȳþed licgan;
hwīlum hongige   hyrstum frætwed,
wlitig, on wāge,   þǣr weras drincað;
frēolic fyrdsceorp   hwīlum folcwigan
wicge wegað   (þonne ic winde sceal
sincfāg swelgan   of sumes bōsme);
hwīlum ic gereordum   rincas laðige
wlonce tō wīne;   hwīlum wrāþum sceal
stefne mīnre   forstolen hreddan,
flȳman fēondsceaþan.   Frige hwæt ic hātte.

HORN

Riddle 14

WEAPONED WARRIOR WAS I.
Now enwraps me the proud
young home-dweller with silver and gold,
carved twisted wires. Sometimes men kiss me;
sometimes with song I summon to battle
kind comrades; sometimes the steed bears
me over the breakers, bright with ornaments;
sometimes a maid fills my
ring-adorned bosom; sometimes I must on the boards,
hard and headless, lie stripped;
sometimes hang, decked with treasures,
fair on the walls, where warriors drink;
a noble war-weapon. Heroes sometimes
bear me on horseback; then I must breath
draw from a bosom, gleaming with gold;
sometimes with my voice I summon warriors
proud to wine; sometimes I must from foes
rescue spoil, with my tongue,
rout plundering robbers. Ask what I am called.

80.

Ic eom æþelinges   eaxlgestealla,
fyrdrinces gefara,   frēan mīnum lēof,
cyninges geselda.   Cwēn mec hwīlum
hwītloccedu hond   on legeð,
eorles dohtor,   þēah hīo æþelu sȳ.
Hæbbe mē on bōsme   þæt on bearwe gewēox.
Hwīlum ic on wloncum   wicge rīde
herges on ende :   heard is mīn tunge.
Oft ic wōðboran   wordlēana sum
āgyfe æfter giedde.   Good is mīn wīse,
꜇ ic sylfa salo.   Saga hwæt ic hātte.

 AM AN AETHLING'S
shoulder-supporter,
a warrior's comrade, loved of my lord,
a king's companion. Me, sometimes, his queen,
white-locked, her hand lays upon,
a nobleman's daughter, though well-born she be.
I have on my breast what grew in the grove.
Sometimes I ride upon a proud steed
at the head of the army; harsh is my tongue.
Often the poet reward for his words I
give after his lay. My manner is good
and I myself sallow. Say what I'm called.

10.

Neb wæs mīn on nearwe,   ⁊ ic neoþan wætre,
flōde, underflōwen,   firgenstrēamum
swīþe besuncen;   ⁊ on sunde āwōx
ufan ȳþum þeaht,   ānum getenge
līþendum wuda   līce mīne;
hæfde feorh cwico,   þā ic of tæðmum cwōm
brimes ⁊ bēames   on blacum hrægl[e].
Sume wǣron hwīte   hyrste mīne,
þā mec lifgende   lyft upp āhōf,
wind of wǣge;   siþþan wīde bær
ofer seolhbaþo.   Saga hwæt ic hātte.

Riddle 10

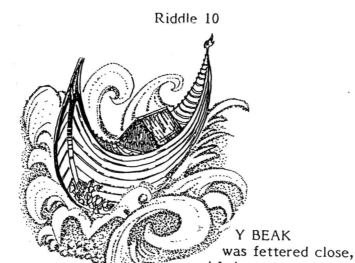

Y BEAK
was fettered close,
and I the current neath,
the flood that under flowed, the primordial streams
deep sunk, grew in the sea,
wrapped by the waves above, alone,
my body nestling up to barks.
All alive was I, when from the clasp I came
of sea and ship, in bright gear clad;
my trappings white in part,
living, when the air raised me aloft,
from the wave, bore widely afterwards
across the seal's-bath. Say what I am called.

16.

Oft ic sceal wiþ wǣge winnan ⁊ wiþ winde feohtan;
somod wiðð þām sæcce, þonne ic sēcan gewīte
eorþan ȳþum þeaht : · mē biþ se ēþel fremde.
Ic bēom strong þæs gewinnes, gif ic stille weorþe;
gif mē þæs tōsǣleð, hī bēoð swīþran þonne ic
⁊ mec slītende sōna flȳmað ;
willað opfergan · þæt ic friþian sceal.
Ic him þæt forstonde, gif mīn steort þolað
⁊ mec stīþne wiþ stānas mōton
fæste gehabban. Frige hwæt ic hātte.

88

FT MUST I WAGE WAR
against wave and fight against wind,
do battle with both, when I set off to seek
the earth, buried by billows; strange is the land to me.
Strong in the struggle am I, if they stay still;
if in that I succeed not, they are stronger than I
and straightway with rending, they put me to rout;
away would they carry what I would keep safe.
Them I withstand, if my tail still endures
and strongly against me the stones are well able
to hold fast. Ask what I'm called.

22.

Ætsomne cwōm   LX monna
to wǣgstæþe   wicgum rīdan;
hæfdon XI   ēoredmæcgas
frīdhengestas,   IIII scēamas.
Ne meahton magorincas   ofer mere fēolan,
swā hī fundedon;   ac wæs flōd tō dēop,
atol ȳþa geþræc,   ōfras hēa,
strēamas stronge.   Ongunnon stīgan þā
on wægn weras,   ⁊ hyra wicg somod
hlōdan under hrunge.   þā þā hors oðbær,
eh ⁊ eorlas   æscum dealle,
ofer wætres byht   wægn tō lande:
swā hine oxa ne tēah,   ne esna mægen,
ne fæt hengest,   ne on flōde swom,
ne be grunde wōd   gestum under,
ne lagu drēfde,   ne o[n] lyfte flēag,
ne [u]nder bæc cyrde;   brōhte hwæþre
beornas ofer burnan   ⁊ hyra bloncan mid
from stæðe hēaum,   þæt hȳ stōpan ūp
on ōþerne   ellenrōfe
weras of wǣge   ⁊ hyra wicg gesund.

90

IXTY MEN TOGETHER CAME
to the seashore riding steeds;
eleven of the horsemen had
stately steeds, four white.
The champions could not cross the mere,
as they discovered, for the flood was deep,
the waves' press dire, the edges steep,
the currents strong. Commenced to climb
the wagon then, the warriors, and their horses too,
loaded underneath the pole; a cob then led away
the steeds and proud men with their ashen spears,
the wagon over the waters' home to land;
yet, neither ox drew it, nor asses' might,
nor sturdy steed; nor did it swim the flood,
nor crawl upon the ground beneath its guests,
nor did it stir the sea, nor fly aloft,
nor turn back; yet, it brought
the warriors on the wave and their white steeds
                              with them
the sheer shore from, so that they stepped upon
the other bank, brave ones,
men from the main and their steeds sound.

27.

Ic eom weorð werum,   wīde funden,
brungen of bearwum   ⁊ of burghleoþu*m*,
of denum ⁊ of dūnum.   Dæges mec wǣgun
feþre on lifte,   feredon mid liste
under hrōfes hlēo.   Hæleð mec siþþan
baþedan in bydene.   Nū ic eom bindere
⁊ swingere,   sōna weorpere;
efne tō eorþan   hwīlum ealdne ceorl.
Sōna þ*æt* onfindeð,   sē þe mec fēhð ongēan
⁊ wið mægenþisan   mīnre genǣsteð,
þæt hē hrycge sceal   hrūsan sēcan,
gif hē unrǣdes   ǣr ne geswīceð;
strengo bīstolen,   strong on sprǣce,
mægene bīnumen,   nāh his mōdes geweald,
fōta ne folma.   Frige hwæt ic hātte,
ðe on eorþan swā   esnas binde
dole æfter dyntum   be dæges lēohte.

FAVOURITE OF MEN AM I,
found far and wide,
from groves fetched and from city-slopes,
from dales and from downs. By day was I borne
aloft upon wings, wafted with skill
under the shelter of roofs. Later by men was I
bathed in a butt. Now a binder am I
and scourge; straightway I cast
to earth a youth, an old man, at times.
Soon he discovers who disputes with me
and struggles against my strength,
that he on his back must fall flat to the ground,
if he flees not his folly before.
Robbed of his strength, though bold of speech,
deprived of his might, nor mastery of mind has he,
nor feet, nor hands. Ask what I call myself
who thus binds servants to the soil,
foolish after fighting, by the light of day.

28.

Biþ foldan dæl   fægre gegierwed
mid þȳ heardestan   ꝺ mid þȳ scearpestan
ꝺ mid þȳ grymmestan   gumena gestrēona.
Corfen, sworfen,   cyrred, þyrred,
bunden, wunden,   blæced, wæced,
frætwed, geatwed,   feorran læded
tō durum dryhta,   drēam biðin innan
cwicra wihta.   Clengeð lengeð
þāra þe ær lifgende   longe hwīle
wilna brūceð,   ꝺ nō wið spriceð;
ꝺ þonne æfter dēaþe   dēman onginneð,
meldan mislīce.   Micel is tō hycganne
wīsfæstum menn,   hwæt sēo wiht sȳ.

 PART OF THE SOIL
is prettily swathed
in the sternest and sharpest
and grimmest of men's gains,
cut, cleaned, turned, dried,
bound, wound, bleached, weakened,
adorned, arrayed, carried away
to the doors of men. Delight is within
for sentient beings; it stays, delays,
among those who living a long while before
savour their pleasures and speak not against it;
and then after death fall to declaiming
with manifold mouthings. 'Tis much to determine
for wise men what that wight be.

32.

Is þes middangeard   missenlicum
wīsum gewlitegad,   wrǣttum gefrætwad.
Sīþum sellic   ic seah searo hweorfan,
grindan wið grēote,   giellende faran.
Næfde sellicu wiht   sȳne ne folme,
exle ne earmas ;   sceal on ānum fēt
searocēap swīfan,   swīþe fēran,
faran ofer feldas ;   hæfde fela ribba ;
mūð wæs on middan.   Moncynne nyt
fer foddurwelan   folcscipe drēogeð,
wist in wigeð,   ꝼ werum gieldeð
gaful gēara gehwām   þæs þe guman brūcað
rīce ꝼ hēane.   Rece, gif þū cunne,
wīs worda glēaw,   hwæt sīo wiht sīe.

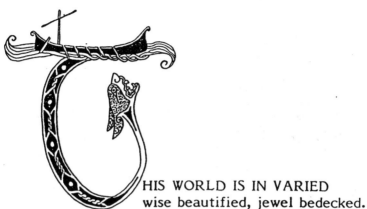

HIS WORLD IS IN VARIED
wise beautified, jewel bedecked.
I saw this creature turn, marvellous in motion,
grind against the gravel, fare groaning.
Nor sight nor hands had this wondrous wight,
nor shoulders nor arms; on one foot it had
to move, the strange one, stir strongly,
fare over fields. Ribs it had many;
midway its mouth was set. Useful to men,
provision in plenty, to people it brings,
bears food within, and renders to folk
tribute each year which all enjoy,
rich and poor alike. Relate if thou canst,
skilled in wise words, what this wight be.

Riddle 46

A WARRIOR SAT AT WINE
with his two wives
and his two sons and daughters two,
sisters fond, and their two sons,
goodly first-born; there the father was
of both these noble ones and each
an uncle and a nephew. Five in all
were sitting there of men and maids.

Wær sæt æt wīne,   mid his wīfum twām,
꒞ his twēgen suno   ꒞ his twā dohtor,
swāse gesweostor,   ꒞ hyr[a] suno twēgen,
frēolico frumbearn;   fæder wæs þærinne
þāra æþelinga   æghwæðres mid,
ēam ꒞ nefa.   Ealra wæron fīfe
eorla ꒞ idesa   insittendra.

98

ARRIED INTO THE HOUSE
saw I captives
under the hall-roof, the hardy pair
that were fellows, with shackles straight
together were fettered fast.
Close to one of them was
a dark-skinned slave who curbed
both in their course with bonds confined.

Ic seah ræpingas   in ræced fergan,
under hrōf sales,   hearde twēgen ;
þā wǣron gen[u]mne,   nearwum bendum,
gefeterade   fæste tōgædre.
þāra ōþrum wæs   ān getenge
·wonfāh Wāle,   sēo wēold hyra
bēga sīþe   bendum fæstra.

Riddle 74

WAS A YOUNG VIRGIN,
a fair-haired woman
and peerless warrior at the same time;
I flew with fowl and swam in the flood,
dived neath the wave, and was dead among fish,
and stepped upon land, a living soul had.

Ic wæs fǣmne geong,   feaxhār cwene
˥ ǣnlic rinc   on āne tīd;
flēah mid fuglum   ˥ on flōde swom,
dēaf under ȳþe   dēad mid fiscum
˥ on foldan stōp;.   hæfde f[e]rð cwicu.

Y HOME IS NOT HUSHED,
nor I myself loud;
... for us two the Lord ordained
our passage together; I'm swifter than he,
stronger at times, he the more steadfast.
Sometimes I rest whereas he must run on.
Ever I dwell in him while I endure;
if we two divide, for me death is destined.

Nis mīn sele swīge   ne ic sylfa hlūd
ymb . . . . . ;   unc Driht[en] scōp
sīþ ætsomne.   Ic eom swi[f]tre þon*ne* hē,
þrāgum strengra,   hē þreohtīgra;
hwīlum ic mē reste,   hē sceal yrnan forð.
Ic him in wunige   ā þenden ic lifge;
gif wit unc gedǣlað,   mē bið dēað witod.

86.

Wiht cwōm gongan,   þǣr weras sǣton
monige on mæðle   mōde snottre;
hæfde ān ēage   ⁊ ēaran twā
⁊ II fēt,   XII hund hēafda,
hryc[g] ⁊ wombe   ⁊ honda twā,
earmas ⁊ eaxle,   ānne swēoran
⁊ sīdan twā.   Saga hwæt ic hātte.

CREATURE CAME
where warriors sat
in council, many wise in mind;
two ears and one eye had it,
two feet and twelve hundred heads,
back and belly and two hands,
arms and shoulders and one neck
and two sides. Say what I am called.

24.

Ic eom wunderlicu wiht;   wrǣsne mīne stefne:
hwīlum beorce swā hund,   hwīlum blǣte swā gāt,
hwīlum grǣde swā gōs,   hwīlum gielle swā hafoc;
hwīlum ic onhyrge   þone haswan earn,
gūðfugles hlēoþor;   hwīlum glidan reorde
mūþe gemǣne,   hwīlum mǣwes song,
þǣr ic glado sitte.   · ᚷ · mec nemnað,
swylce · ᚾ · ᚷ · ᚱ ·; · ᚠ · fullesteð
· ᚻ · ᚷ · ᛁ ·.   Nū ic hāten eom
swā þā siex stafas   sweotule bēcnaþ.

RUNES

Riddle 24

AM A WONDROUS WIGHT:
                    I vary my voice:
     at times I bark like a dog,
            at times I bleat like a goat,
       at times I cry like a goose,
            at times I yell like a hawk,
at times the grey eagle I imitate,
the sound of the war-bird; at times the kite's speech
to my mouth is familiar, at times the mew's song,
where I sit glad. G names me,
likewise A and R; O helps
H and I. Now am I named
as these six symbols clearly show.

42.

Ic seah wyhte   wrǣtlice twā
undearnunga   ūte plegan
hǣmedlāces :   hwītloc anfeng
wlanc under wǣdum,   gif þæs weorces spēo[w],
fǣmne fyllo.   Ic on flette mæg
þurh rūnstafas   rincum secgan,
þām þe bēc witan,   bēga ætsomne
naman þāra wihta.   þǣr sceal Nȳd wesan
twēga ōþer   ⁊ se torhta Æsc
ān an līnan,   Ācas twēgen,
Hǣgelas swā some,   hwylc [þ]æs hordgates.
cǣgan cræfte   þā clamme onlēac,
þe þā rǣdellan   wið rȳnemenn
hygefæste hēold   heortan, bewrigene
orþoncbendum.   Nū' is undyrne
werum æt wīne,   hū þā wihte mid ūs
hēan mōde twā   hātne sindon.

Riddle 42

WO CURIOUS CREATURES
saw I
openly indulge outside
in sexual love; the white-locked took,
beneath her weeds, if that work prospered, proud,
a virgin's fill. I can, upon the floor,
with runic letters, warriors tell,
men who understand books, both
those creatures' names. There shall NYD be
in each of two, and the excellent AESC
one on the line, of AC two,
of HAEGL likewise. Which key's skill was it
unlocked the chains of that hoard's gates
which the riddle from rune-men
wisely held, hid in their heart
with cunningly-contrived bonds? Now is revealed
to warriors at their wine how those wights with us
the mean-minded pair, are called.

Riddle 64

SAW W AND I OVER
the field fare,
bearing B E; for both on that trip was
H and A the holder's delight,
a share of such strength. TH and E
rejoiced; F and A flew over EA
S and P of that folk itself.

Ic seah · ᛈ · ᛄ · ᛁ ·   ofer wong faran,
beran · ᛒ · · ᛗ ·;   bǣm wæs on siþþe
hæbbendes hyht, ᚾ · ᛄ · ᚼ ·
swylce þrȳþa dǣl,   · ᚦ · ᛄ · ᛗ ·
Gefeah · ᚹ · ᛄ · ᚠ ·,   fleah ofer · ᛇ ·;
· ᚻ · ᛄ · ᚻ ·   sylfes þæs folces.

108

OBSCENE

Riddle 25

ONDROUS A WIGHT AM I,
to women a joy;
to neighbours of use; I injure none
in cities that dwell, save slayers alone.
Lofty my state, I stand over the bed,
shaggy somewhere below. Sometimes attempts,
handsome and young, a peasant's vile daughter,
proud virgin, to take possession of me;
rushes on me, red, plunders my head,
fast fixes on me. Straightway she feels
what meeting me means, when she molests me,
the curly-haired woman. Wet is that eye.

Ic eom wunderlicu wiht,   wīfum on hyhte,
nēahbūendum nyt;   nǣngum sceþþe
burgsittendra,   nymþe bonan ānum.
Staþol mīn is stēap,   hēah stonde ic on bedde,
neoþan rūh, nāthwǣr.   Nēþeð hwīlum
ful cyrtenu. ceorles dohtor,
mōdwlonc mēowle,   þæt hēo on mec grīpeð,
rǣseð mec on rēodne,   rēafað mīn hēafod,
fēgeð mec on fæsten;   fēleþ sōna
mīnes gemōtes   sē[o] þe mec nearwað,
wīf wundenlocc :   wǣt bið þæt ēage.

109

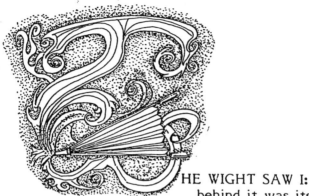

HE WIGHT SAW I:
behind it was its womb
dilated huge. A thane attacked it,
a mighty man, and much had he
endured when through its eye what filled it flew.
It does not always die when it must yield
its vitals to another, but there comes again
reward into its bosom, breath returns;
a son it generates; its very father 'tis.

Ic þā wihte geseah; womb wæs on hindan
þrīþum āþrunten. Þegn folgade,
mægenrōfa man, Ᵹ micel hæfde
gefēred þær [þæt] hit f[y]lde flēah þurh his ēage.
Ne swylteð hē symle þonne syllan sceal
innað þām ōþrum, ac him eft cymeð
bōt in bōsme, blæd biþ ārēred;
hē sunu wyrceð, bið him sylfa fæder.

110

Riddle 44

UPON THE husband's thigh it splendid hangs,
the consort's cloak beneath. An orifice in front.
Stiff and hard it is and has a goodly stand;
when his own dress the youth
lifts up above his knee, he likes that well-known hole
his hangar's head to greet,
so that he fill it whole as once he often did.

Wrætlic hongað   bī weres þēo,
frēan under scēate;   foran is þ̄yrel;
bið stīþ Ᵹ heard,   stede hafað gōdne.
Þonne se esne   his āgen hrægl
ofer cnēo hefeð,   wile þæt cūþe hol
mid his hangellan   hēafde grētan,
þæt hē efelang ǣr   oft gefylde.

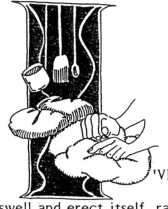

'VE HEARD OF SOMETHING
wax in a corner,
swell and erect itself, raise up its covers;
fondled that boneless thing the bride
proudly with hands, hid with her garment,
the sovereign's daughter, that swelling thing.

Ic on wincle gefrægn   w.[āces] nāthwæt
þindan ꞇ þunian,   þecene hebban.
On þæt bānlēase   brȳd grāpode
hygewlonc hondum;   hrægle þeahte
þ[i]ndende þing   þēodnes dohtor.

112

Riddle 54

ALKING A YOUTH CAME,
to where he knew she
stood in a corner; towards her he strode,
a lusty bachelor; lifted her own
garment with his hands, thrust under her girdle
something inflexible as she stood there;
wrought his desire; together they trembled.
Hastened the thane, useful at times.
A capable servant, he tired nonetheless,
with every respite, though robust before,
weary of that work. To wax then began
beneath her girdle what good men oft
heartily cherish and purchase with coin.

Hyse cwōm gangan,　þǣr hē hīe wisse
stondan in wī[n]sele;　stōp feorran tō
hrōr hægstealdmon,　hōf his āgen
hrægl hondum ūp,　h[r]and under gyrdels
hyre stondendre　stīþes nāthwæt,
worhte his willan;　wagedan būta.
þegn onnette,　wæs þrāgum nyt,
tillic esne;　teorode hwæþre
æt stunda gehwām　strong ǣr þon[ne] hīe ō,
wērig þæs weorces.　Hyre weaxan ongon
under gyrdelse　þæt oft gōde men
ferðþum frēogað　ꝥ mid fēo bicgað.

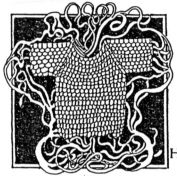

HE FAIR MAID OFT
             immures me fast,
within a chest; the woman me withdrew sometimes
with her own hands and gave me to her lord,
her gracious prince, as she was bid.
Then thrust he deep his head into
me upwards from below, into that narrow part.
If the strength of that attack availed,
adorned as I was there should fill
me something rough. Guess what I mean.

Oft mec fæste bīlēac   frēolicu mēowle,
ides on earce;   hwīlum up ātēah
folmum sīnum   ⁊ frēan sealde,
holdum þēodne,   swā hīo hāten wæs.
Siðþan mē on hreþre   hēafod sticade;
nioþan ūpweardne   on nearo fēgde.
Gif þæs ondfengan   ellen dohte,
þe mec frætwed[e],   fyllan sceolde
rūwes nāthwæt.   Rǣd hwæt ic mǣne.

Riddle 62

'M HARD AND SHARP,
in entry strong,
departure bold, deserving of my lord,
the womb I enter from below, myself the way
rightly enlarge. The hero is in haste,
who from behind belabours me,
the champion, with his dream; he draws me out at times
hot from the hole; at times I fare again
into the narrow part somewhere; he presses hard,
the southern man. Say what I'm called.

Ic eom heard ꞓ scearp,   [h]ingonges strong,
forðsiþes from,   frēan unforcūð;
wade under wambe   ꞓ me weg syıra
ryhtne gerȳme.   Rinc bið on ofeste,
sē mec on þȳð   æftanweardne,
hæleð mid hrægle;   hwīlum ūt tȳhð
of hole hātne;   hwīlum eft fare [ic]
on nearo nāthwǣr;   nȳdeþ swīþe
sūþerne secg.   Saga hwæt ic hātte.

SUGGESTED SOLUTIONS

1 Storm on Land (W)
2 Submarine Earthquake (S)
4 Bell (M)
5 Shield (A)
6 Sun (M)
7 Swan (H)
8 Jay (T)
9 Cuckoo (I)
10 Goose Barnacle (M)
11 Wine (G)
12 Oxhide (I)
13 Ten Chickens (T)
14 Horn (A)
15 Badger (W)
16 Anchor (O)
17 Ballista (T)
21 Plough (M)
22 Circling Stars (S)
23 Bow (A)
24 Magpie (I)
25 Onion (W)
26 Bible-Codex (A)
27 Mead (A)
28 Harp (A)
29 Sun and Moon (A)
31 Bagpipe (T)
32 Ship (T)
33 Iceberg (W)
34 Rake (I)
35 Mail-Shirt (M)
37 Bellows (T)
38 Young Bull (A)
39 Hypostasized Death (W)
42 Cock and Hen (T)
43 Soul and Body (A)
44 Key (U)

45 Dough (I)
46 Lot and his Family (A)
47 Book Moth (A)
48 Chalice (I)
49 Oven (O)
50 Fire (W)
51 Pen and Three Fingers (I)
52 Flail (C)
54 Churn (W)
55 Scabbard and Cross (I)
56 Weaver's Loom (I)
57 Swallows (S)
58 Draw-well (A)
61 Mail-shirt (T)
62 Poker (I)
64 Man on Horseback with Hawk (I)
65 Onion (A)
66 Creation (G)
70 Shepherd's Pipe (W)
74 Siren (I)
80 Horn (I)
85 Fish and River (N)
86 One-eyed Garlic Seller (A)
91 Key (M).

Also published by
Llanerch:

BEOWULF
translated by John Porter
with drawings by Nicholas Parry

AN ANGLO-SAXON GENESIS
Genesis 'A' translated by Lawrence Mason
with the drawings from the Junius Ms.

NORTHUMBRIAN CROSSES
by W. G. Collingwood

LIVES OF THE
NORTHUMBRIAN SAINTS
by S. Baring-Gould

SYMBOLISM OF THE
CELTIC CROSS
by Derek Bryce

BARDS AND HEROES
by Carl Lofmark

THE BLACK BOOK
OF CARMARTHEN
translated by Meirion Pennar

For a complete list,
write to:
LLANERCH ENTERPRISES,
Felinfach, Lampeter,
Dyfed. SA48 8PJ.